A HORRID FACTBOOK

HORRID HENRY'S ANIMALS

Francesca Simon

Illustrated by Tony Ross

Orion
Children's Books

First published in Great Britain in 2014
by Orion Children's Books
a division of the Orion Publishing Group Ltd
Orion House
5 Upper Saint Martin's Lane
London WC2H 9EA
An Hachette UK company

1 3 5 7 9 10 8 6 4 2

Facts compiled by Sally Byford.

The Orion Publishing Group's policy is to use papers that are natural, renewable
and recyclable products and made from wood grown in sustainable forests.
The logging and manufacturing processes are expected to conform to the
environmental regulations of the country of origin.

ISBN 978 1 4440 1149 4

A catalogue record for this book is available from the British Library.

Printed in Great Britain by
Clays Ltd, St Ives plc

www.orionbooks.co.uk

www.horridhenry.co.uk

CONTENTS

Hello from Henry

Hi gang!

Animals! Yeah, we're talking about REAL animals, not walking dusters like Fat Fluffy. Mum and Dad won't let me have a snake or a crocodile – it's so unfair! But a person can dream, can't he, about blood-squirting horned lizards and deadly black mambas and sixteen tonne elephants squishing Miss Battle-Axe . . . Happy reading! And look out for golden poison dart frogs.

Henry

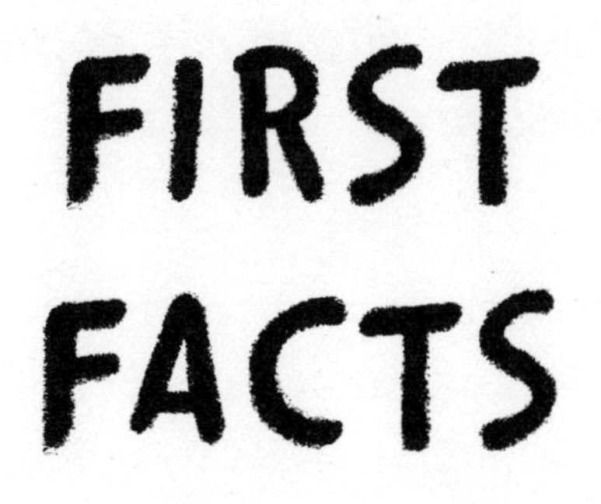
FIRST
FACTS

The amazing animals in this book come from five families: **mammals**, **reptiles**, **amphibians**, **birds** and **fish**.

Mammals come in all shapes and sizes – from a shrew so small it can fit on a teaspoon, to a whale so huge that its tongue weighs more than an elephant – but they all have **hair**, feed their babies **milk**, and have **warm blood**.

Reptiles have **scaly skin** and **cold blood**, which they warm up in the sun.

Just like Margaret.

Amphibians live in the water when they are young and live on land as adults. For example, tadpoles turn into frogs **(and Margarets)**. Their skin is **smooth**, without any scales, feathers or fur. Like reptiles they have **cold blood**.

Birds are warm-blooded with **feathers** and **wings**. Most birds use their wings for flying, but some birds, like ostriches, can't fly because their wings are too small and weak.

Fish swim in lakes, rivers or the sea, and have **cold blood**.

Today there are around

5,000 different types of **mammals**

7,000 kinds of **amphibians** **(Make that 7,002, including frog-face Margaret and Peter the toad.)**

10,000 types of **reptiles**

10,000 kinds of **birds**

. . . and **30,000** types of **fish**.

That's a grand total of over **60,000** kinds of animals.

MEGA-MONSTERS AND MINI-BEASTS . . .

A **blue whale's** heart is huge! It's the same size as a **small car**, with blood vessels big enough for a child to crawl through.

Newborn **blue whale babies** weigh nearly **three tonnes** and drink over **200 litres of milk** a day – as much as 100 bottles of fizzywizz.

That's more than Greedy Graham.

Kitti's hog-nosed bat, also called the bumblebee bat, is probably the **world's smallest mammal**. It's only about 3 cm long and could sit on the end of your finger.

Polar bears have very big feet, up to 30 cm wide – about the size of a dinner plate – to support their great weight on the snow and ice.

Everyone knows that birds make **cosy nests**, but did you know that **gorillas** do too? They build great big ones on the ground from plants like nettles and giant celery.

At only 12 cm long, the **pygmy marmoset** from the Amazon rainforest is the **world's smallest monkey**.

The **red-eyed tree frog** is only 5-7 cm long, so small it could sit on the end of a pencil like a **pencil topper**.

When a **grizzly bear** stands up on its hind legs, it's the same height as you would be if you stood on your dad's shoulders.

The **leaf chameleon** from Madagascar looks just like a full-sized chameleon shrunk down to the size of an adult's thumbnail.

The **white rhinoceros** is four times as heavy as a family car, but it's a **gentle giant** and runs away from people rather than attacking them.

Seahorses have just one tiny back fin to propel them through the water, which makes them very **slow swimmers** – moving only 2 metres in an hour.

Ostriches are the **biggest birds in the world** and their eggs can be up to **20 cm** long – about the size of a large mango.

The **wandering albatross** is a **giant seabird** with the largest wingspan of any flying animal – up to 3.6 metres – almost four times the width of your outstretched arms.

The **bee hummingbird** is just 6 cm long. It weighs less than a few grains of rice, and its eggs are the size of a **pea**.

The **whale shark** is the biggest fish in the world, weighing more than 20 tonnes – the same weight as **two school buses** full of children.

GROSS-OUT

Gorillas never stop **farting**! All the vegetables they eat give them wind. One zoo had to ban all sprouts when visitors complained that the stink was **even stinkier** than usual.

Wow.

When a **skunk** is threatened, it arches its back and lifts its tail to make itself look big and scary. If that doesn't work, it squirts a **stinky fluid** from under its tail. **Gross**!

Indian rhinos mark their territory with **piles of poo**. That's because rhinos have a much better **sense of smell** than they do sight, and the poo helps them find their way home!

Vampire bats feed on **fresh blood**. They creep across the ground, sniffing for **prey**, like horses or cows, or even human beings, then they **bite** their victim and lap up the blood.

Yikes. Maybe I could point one towards Miss Battle-Axe.

Very young **koala** babies snuggle in their mum's pouch and **feed on her poo**, before they start eating eucalyptus like she does.

Yuck.

Monkeys groom one another's fur to keep themselves nice and clean. And they **eat** the lice they find along the way!

Better than Nitty Nora Bug Explorer.

Male **orang-utans** like to live alone and they **burp** very loudly to warn other males away.

When a **camel** is **angry** or **frightened**, it spits out **rotten juice** which comes straight up from its stomach. **Bleccch**.

Roadrunners lay around **eight eggs** at a time – that's a lot of hungry chicks. And if they can't feed all their babies, they **eat** the smallest one.

Desert-dwelling frogs and **toads** burrow **underground** and cover themselves in their own **mucus** while they wait for rain. They can stay like this for ***years***.

Hedgehogs aren't very good at keeping clean – their spikes can hide more than **1,000 fleas**!

GOBBLE AND GO

Imagine only eating **once a week**. **Lions** scoff so much in one meal that they don't eat again for five or six days.

I don't think Greedy Graham would make a great lion.

Elephants need to eat **300 kg** of plants, a pile as big as a **garden shed**, and drink more than a **bathful** of water every day.

On a hot summer's night, a **bat** gobbles between **3,000** to **7,000** mosquitoes – that's about **600** an hour!

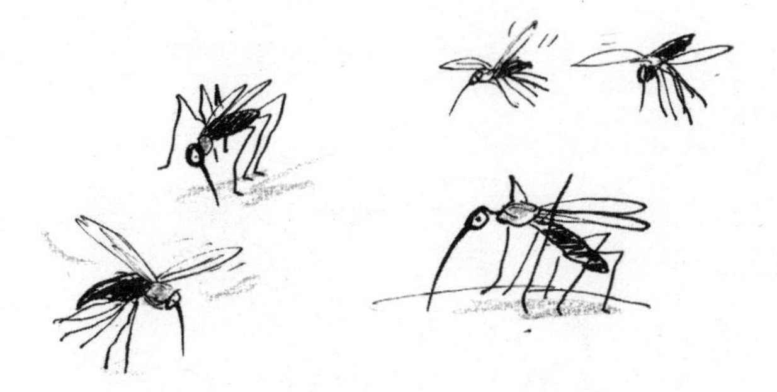

It takes **1,000 kg** of food to fill up a **blue whale's** stomach.

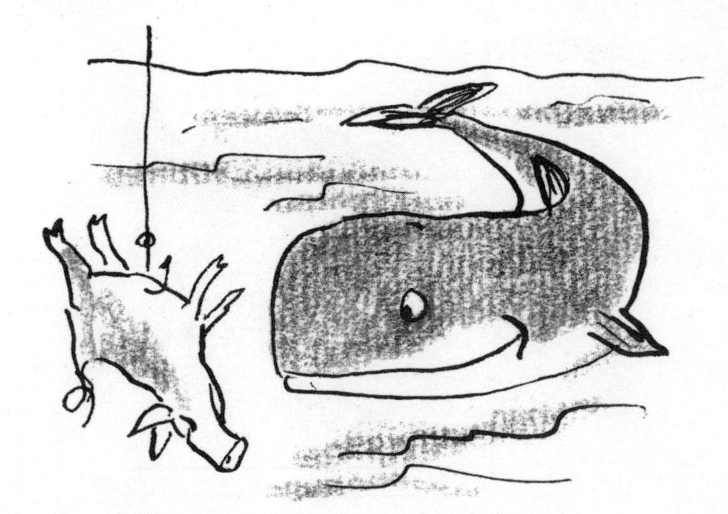

The **Tasmanian devil** will eat **anything**. It crushes **bones** with its teeth and eats its prey **whole** – fur, feathers and all!

The **giant anteater** doesn't have any teeth – instead, it uses its 60 cm tongue to sweep ants from their nest into its mouth, eating up to **30,000** in one day.

Bet it wishes it could have a pizza instead.

Squirrels hide **hundreds of nuts** before they hibernate for the winter, but when they wake up they can't remember where they have hidden half of them. The nuts grow into **trees** instead.

Horrible **hagfish** can be found lurking at the bottom of the sea. They are so thin they can slither inside the bodies of their prey and eat them from the **inside out**.

Pandas are **picky eaters** – the only thing they really like to eat is bamboo. Luckily, their stomachs have a **tough lining** to protect them, so they don't get splinters from the wood.

The ***aye-aye*** – a type of lemur – loves **gobbling grubs**, and has a special way of trapping them. It taps on tree trunks and listens for grubs moving about, then it rips away the bark with its teeth and hooks them out with its extra-long middle finger.

The **anaconda** snake doesn't have teeth, so it **swallows its prey whole**. It can gulp down mice, fish, birds and even deer by unhinging its jaws to stretch its mouth around its prey.

Hmm . . . I wonder if I should give one to Peter.

Moles walk along their underground tunnels and eat earthworms that have fallen in. Sometimes they just **bite off their heads** and save the rest to snack on later.

A **chameleon's tongue** is nearly twice the length of its body, with a **super-sticky** tip. It shoots in and out to catch insects so fast that you don't see it happening.

POWERFUL PREDATORS

Predators are meat-eating animals like lions, eagles and killer sharks that **hunt**, **kill** and **eat** other animals.

Scavengers, like vultures and hyenas, also like eating meat, but they leave the hunting to the predators and eat their **leftovers** later.

In a pride of lions, it's the **lionesses** that do **90%** of the hunting. They creep up on their prey in packs and form a semi-circle around their food so it **can't escape**.

Tigers hunt alone. They sneak through the undergrowth, before **leaping out** and **attacking** their victims.

Killer whales are the ocean's top predators. They hunt in groups and use their **long teeth** to kill seals and fish.

The **great white shark** attacks seals, dolphins and even **small boats**, bashing them with its snout until they sink.

The **harpy eagle** can spot a monkey from 3 km away. It swoops at **lightning speed** and snatches the monkey out of its tree with its talons.

Sharks can smell **blood** from 5 km away.

Piranha fish attack in groups. They work together, using their tiny triangular teeth, to strip an animal **to the bone** in minutes.

The **hammerhead shark** has an eye on each side of its head, so it can spot prey from **all directions**.

Leopards drag animals they have killed into the **branches of trees** to eat, keeping them safely away from hyenas who might want to steal their lunch!

If you spot a **spitting cobra**, beware. This scary snake raises its head, spreads its hood and shoots **venom** straight into the eyes of its victim.

Pythons and **boa constrictors** wrap their enormous bodies around their prey and **squeeze tight** until the prey chokes to death.

One bite from a **king cobra** can release enough **venom** to kill an elephant.

The **alligator snapping turtle** lurks at the bottom of a lake with its mouth wide open. Its pink **wriggly tongue** looks like a **worm**, so when fish come to investigate, the turtle snaps its mouth shut and eats them.

Polar bears' feet are tipped with claws that can rip a seal's belly open, and their powerful jaws can crush a seal's skull in one bite.

Hmm. All this biting and chewing is making me hungry. Chocolate Gooey Chewy anyone?

SURVIVAL

Horned lizards squirt foul-tasting blood out of their **eyes** at their attackers.

Yeah! I'm putting one on my list for Father Christmas right now.

When a **hedgehog** is threatened, it rolls into a ball and makes the **6,000 sharp spines** on its back stand on end.

Ostriches can outrun most attackers – they can get up to speeds of **70 km per hour**.

Hmm. I wonder if Aerobic Al could beat one.

Armadillos have hundreds of small, hard scales all over their bodies, like **armour**, and if they are attacked they quickly roll up into a tight ball.

Cats can survive falls of over **20 metres** – as much as **three giraffes** standing on top of each other.

Meerkats are an **easy target** for predators, so while some of the group hunt for food, others stand on their back legs and tail to act as **lookouts**.

If a **puffer fish** senses danger, it swallows water and swells up like a **balloon** so that its spines stand on end.

Hamsters are well-known for stuffing their cheek pouches with **food**, but mother hamsters sometimes protect their **babies** from danger by hiding them in their cheeks too.

Weird!

Giraffes take a while to stand up from a lying down position, so they only sleep for **two minutes at a time**, standing up.

An **aardvark** can dig a burrow and hide in just **a few seconds**.

Sharks don't give up easily in a fight. They can carry on **attacking** even if their insides have been bitten out and they are **bleeding**.

REMARKABLE REPTILES

Did you know that **snakes** are sometimes born with **two heads**? The heads of a two-headed snake will **fight** each other for food, even though they share the same stomach.

Crocodiles and **alligators** can't stick their tongues out or chew.

Snakes don't have **eyelids** so their eyes stay open **all the time** – even when they're asleep.

The **crested gecko** doesn't have any eyelids either. Luckily it has a **long tongue** to lick all the dirt out of its eyes.

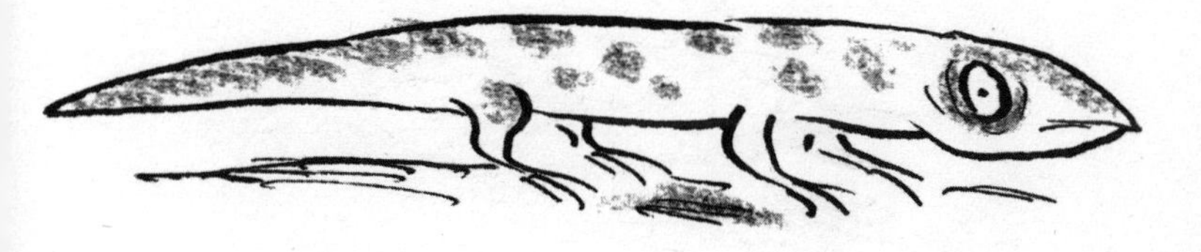

The **thorny devil lizard** lives in the Australian outback where there isn't much water. At night, the lizard collects dew on its body, which runs down the grooves between its spines and straight into its mouth.

Crocodiles and **alligators** can float with only their eyes and nostrils above the water. That's how they **sneak up** on their victims without being spotted.

Some turtles and tortoises, like the **Eastern box turtle**, can live for more than **100 years**.

Yikes! This looks just like Great Aunt Greta.

Male **Nile crocodiles** put on a strange display to try and attract a girlfriend. They roar, thrash their bodies about and shoot water into the air **from their nostrils**.

Snakes smell with their **tongues**. The tongue collects scents from the air and the things it touches, which tells the snake what is around it.

Crocodiles have the strongest bite of all animals – strong enough to **crush a skull** or a turtle's shell in one **crunch**.

. . . but **crocodiles** don't actually bite to kill. Instead, they catch a victim **in their jaws**, pull it into the water and drag it under so that it drowns.

Wonder whether Miss Battle-Axe is going on holiday somewhere with lots of water . . . ?

TRUE OR FALSE?

Goldfish have a memory span of just three seconds, so by the time they've swum round their bowl, they've already forgotten it.

FALSE: Scientists at Plymouth University have discovered that goldfish can be taught simple tricks, like pushing levers. They remember these skills for up to three months.

A chicken can run around even after its head has been chopped off.

TRUE: It will be so scared and excited from being chased that its muscles will carry on twitching, and sometimes its wings will keep flapping too.

Tigers have stripy skin.

TRUE: A tiger's pattern of black stripes is on its skin as well as its fur.

Ostriches bury their heads in the sand when they're scared.

FALSE: Ostriches don't do this, but they do dig holes in the dirt to lay their eggs. They often put their heads down into the hole to turn the eggs over with their beaks.

An elephant never forgets.

TRUE: Elephants have big brains. They remember where to find food and water, and will recognise an old elephant friend even after years apart.

Elephants are scared of mice.

FALSE: Elephants don't often meet mice, and as they don't have very good eyesight they probably wouldn't even notice a mouse, let alone run away from it.

Bulls get angry when they see the colour red.

FALSE: Bulls aren't very good at spotting different colours. At bullfights, it's the matador flapping his cape around which makes the bull angry, not the colour.

You can escape an alligator by running in a zigag.

FALSE: If an alligator comes after you, run in a straight line as fast as you can! Alligators don't like running very far.

I'm not telling Peter that.

Indian cobras dance to the snake charmer's music.

FALSE: Indian cobras can't hear – they follow the snake charmer's movements, not the music.

Chocolate is poisonous to dogs.

TRUE: Chocolate contains a chemical which can make a dog get sick or even die.

Poor dogs. Glad I'm not one. Too bad there's no chemical in vegetables which makes humans sick . . . or is there?

PET TRIVIA

Rats need **super-strong cages** – they can chew through metal, electrical cables and pipes.

Clever cats never get stuck in tight spaces because they use their **whiskers** to check if a space is wide enough for them to fit through.

Fat Fluffy, on the other hand, never gets stuck in tight places because she never moves.

If you want a pet to talk to, get a **grey parrot**. Some of them can say more than **750** words. They can also mimic sounds like **burps** and **farts**.

Golden hamsters aren't as **cute** and **cuddly** as they look – if you put two of them in a cage they fight, sometimes to the **death**.

Don't put your **goldfish** in the dark. They need sunlight to keep the golden colour of their skin.

Ferrets collect things like socks and keys and hide them. This is because, in the wild, they **kill** more animals than they can eat, so they store some away for later.

A **cat's** tongue is **scratchy** because it's lined with **tiny hooks** that help to hold mice and birds in place.

Guinea pigs can recognise when their owners are opening fridge doors or rustling the bags where their food is kept, and they make a funny whistling sound when they know their **lunch** is about to be served.

Ancient Egyptians **loved** their **dogs**. When a dog died, the owners would **shave off** their **eyebrows**, smear mud in their hair and wail for days.

Like all humans, Miss Battle-Axe has around **10,000** facial expressions. Her pet **poodle**, Piddle, has only around **100** expressions, and most of these are made with its **ears**.

Gerbils don't like to **wash** in water. Instead, they roll in sand, which **polishes** their fur.

Cats have **amazing eyesight**. They can see 36 metres away – the same length as three double-decker buses.

In the nineteenth century, a French poet had a very weird pet. It was a **lobster** called Thibault, which he took for walks around Paris on the end of a blue ribbon.

TOP TALENTS

Chimpanzees have been taught to communicate with humans using **sign language**.

Some **polar bears** cover their dark noses with snow when they are hunting seals, so that they are completely white. A clever disguise!

Bloodhounds are brilliant at solving crimes because their sense of smell is **10 million** times better than a human's.

Swallows have amazing memories. They fly thousands of miles during **migration** every year, but often fly back to exactly the same nest they used the year before.

The **mockingbird** can imitate lots of sounds – from ringing telephones to barking dogs, as well as the songs and calls of other birds.

A **chameleon** can swivel its eyes separately to look forwards and backwards at the same time.

Chameleons can also **change colour** – either to hide from attackers or to show what mood they are in.

The tiny **fennec fox** has amazing hearing and its enormous ears can pick up the sound of **one beetle** scurrying across the ground.

Pigs are such clever animals that they can be taught to push a joystick with their **snouts** to play video games.

Owls can't move their eyes like we can – but they *can* **turn their heads** almost all the way around!

Bubbles the monkey belonged to pop star Michael Jackson and learned how to do the **moonwalk** dance, made popular by his famous owner.

The big **black woodpecker** can peck through **15 cm** of solid wood – that's more than the width of a house brick!

Humpback whales sing to each other – but it's the same 30 minute song over and over again.

Boring.

In just one night, a **mole** can dig a tunnel 100 metres long, the same distance as one end of a football pitch to the other.

Male **kangaroos** are **champion fighters**. They stand up on their hind legs and **box** each other with their front paws until one of them falls over.

Gecko lizards have toes with so many ridges, bristles and hairs that they can stick to almost any surface, even walls and ceilings!

TOP TEN UGLIES

(Eleven, counting Peter.)

10

The **X-ray fish's** skin and muscles are completely **transparent** – you can see right through its body.

With its soft brown furry body, stubby tail, four webbed feet and rubbery beak, the Australian **duck-billed platypus** looks like a cross between an **otter** and a **beaver** mixed up with a **duck**!

8 The **proboscis monkey** has a funny long nose with a big round end. The males with the biggest noses are the most **popular** with the females.

7 The **aye-aye** from Madagascar looks like a crazy little **goblin** with long claw-like fingers. It got its name long ago because people cried out "aye-aye" in fear when they saw it.

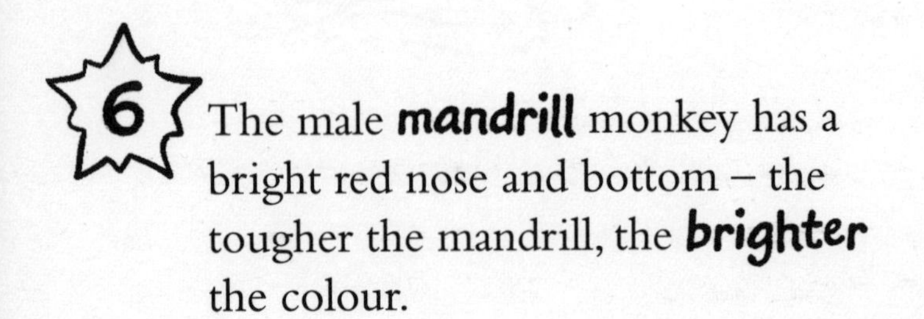

6 The male **mandrill** monkey has a bright red nose and bottom – the tougher the mandrill, the **brighter** the colour.

5 The **Celestial eye goldfish** from China has such large protruding eyeballs that its eyes are bigger than its stomach.

4 An **elephant seal** is fat, grey and clumsy, with a massive floppy trunk – not a pretty sight!

3 Bald and red-faced, the **Californian condor** isn't pretty. And it's bald for a horrible reason – without feathers, it's easier to **stick its head inside** the dead body of its prey.

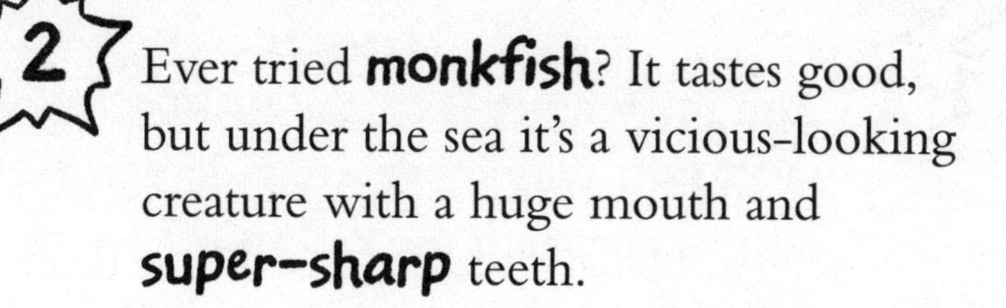

Ever tried **monkfish**? It tastes good, but under the sea it's a vicious-looking creature with a huge mouth and **super-sharp** teeth.

And the winner is . . . the **naked mole rat**, which lives in underground burrows beneath the deserts of eastern Africa. Almost completely hairless, it also has **huge** front teeth.

ANIMAL AEROBICS

Kangaroos are **fantastic jumpers**. They use their long tail like **another leg** to give them an extra push off the ground and they can reach heights of over 3 metres.

Penguins can dive as deep as **400 metres** – the same length as three and a half football pitches.

Male **mudskippers** – a funny sort of fish – show off to females by doing **back-flips** in the air and **push-ups** on their front fins.

Hummingbirds can fly, eat, drink and sleep – all at the same time. They are also the only birds that can **fly backwards**.

Greyhounds are the fastest dogs in the world, running at speeds of **72 km per hour**.

Flying frogs can't actually fly, but they glide from tree to tree using their huge fingers and toes linked together by **webs of skin** as parachutes.

A **basilisk lizard** can run across water – it uses the flaps of skin between each toe to help it stay afloat.

Cats can jump up to five times their own height in one leap.

Fluffy CAN jump . . . hmm, not sure I've ever SEEN her jump though.

Elephants are the only mammals that can't jump, but they can **stand on their heads** – which is something only elephants and humans can do.

When a **zebra** gallops very fast, it takes all four hooves off the ground during every stride so it looks as though it's flying through the air.

Manatees can stay underwater for over 24 minutes. Watch the clock for 24 minutes and you'll realise how long that is!

LONGEST, TALLEST, FASTEST, SMALLEST . . .

Longest – the **royal python**, a super-sized snake which can grow as long as 10 metres, almost the same as a double-decker bus.

Tallest – the giant **giraffe**, measuring up to 6 metres – as high as your house.

Fastest sprinter – the **cheetah** can run at a maximum speed of 110 km per hour for about 30 seconds. That's as quick as a car in the fast lane of the motorway.

Fastest flyer – the **peregrine falcon** can reach speeds of 290 km per hour as it swoops down on its prey.

Fastest swimmer – the **dolphin**, at 56 km per hour – or nearly 19 lengths of a swimming pool in 1 minute!

Smallest – the **bee hummingbird**. Without its feathers, this little bird is smaller and lighter than a bumblebee.

Biggest – the **blue whale** is the largest animal that has ever lived. It can grow as long as 34 metres, the length of four double-decker buses, and weigh 150 tonnes, or more than 21 elephants.

Biggest land animal – the **African elephant**, standing 3.7 metres high, the same height as one fully grown adult standing on the shoulders of another. And it weighs nearly 7 tonnes, which is 80 times as much as an adult man.

Slowest – the **sloth** stays completely still during the day, and at night it creeps along the ground slowly on its stomach, looking for food. It moves so slowly that moss can grow on its fur!

Fattest – the **ringed seal** pup. Half of its body is fat, because it has a thick layer of blubber under its skin to help it keep warm in the Arctic sea.

Largest ears – the **African elephant's** ears measure 1.5 metres each, about the size of a sheet for a double bed.

Brainiest – **human beings**. Yes, even Beefy Bert.

STRANGE BUT TRUE

Little Snowflake, who lived at Barcelona Zoo in Spain from 1996 to 2003, was a very special **gorilla**. He was **white all over**, apart from his bright blue eyes.

Giraffes' tongues are **half a metre long**! They are also bluish-black in colour, which stops them getting sunburned while they eat.

Dalmatian dogs are completely white when they are born. The **spots** appear later.

In the early 1970s, scientists discovered a **camel** which had an amazing **four fully formed humps**, instead of the usual one or two.

The **star-nosed mole** has tiny eyes and is almost **totally blind**. At the end of its nose, the mole has a circle of **22 tentacles**, which move like tiny fingers to help the mole find its way.

Horses and **cows** can sleep standing up.

The horn of a **rhinoceros** isn't made of bone – it's made of packed-together hair.

In the USA, a survey revealed that **33% of dog owners** talk to their pets on the phone while they are away.

Some **mammals** can glide through the air, but **bats** are the only mammals that can actually **fly**.

Pigeons are the only birds that swallow water like we do. Other birds just fill their mouths with water and then tip their heads back.

Lions can't roar until they're two years old.

Cheetahs purr like cats, but the noise is so loud it sounds like a **car engine**.

Bats sleep hanging upside down. They grip onto a surface using their claws and don't let go, even when they're fast asleep.

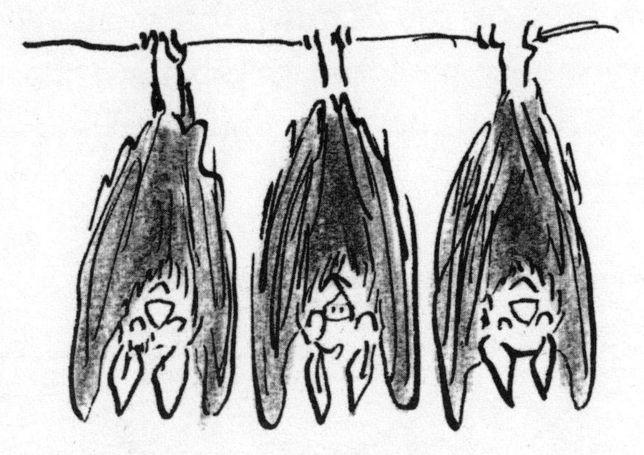

Hippos don't get sunburned. Their skin produces a red, oily liquid which is their very own **sun cream**.

Polar bears are covered in **fluffy white fur**, but their skin is actually **black**.

Dolphins stop breathing if they fall asleep, so they snooze with one eye open, resting at the surface of the water, and switching between eyes.

It's the male **seahorse**, not the female, who carries the eggs until they hatch, in a **pouch** on his stomach.

In the same way that humans can be identified by their unique fingerprints, **dogs** can be identified by their **nose prints**.

Koalas can sleep balanced in the fork of a tree – for up to **18 hours a day.**

WATCH OUT! ANIMALS ABOUT!

One tiny **golden poison dart frog** has enough venom in its body to kill **ten people**.

From 2008 to 2012, **great white sharks** have killed **four humans each year**.

A kick from a **kangaroo** could **kill** a human – so don't get too close!

A **polar bear** can cut off a human head with a swipe of its massive paw.

Every year, 2,000 humans are hunted and drowned by **crocodiles**.

Hippos might look **fat** and **friendly**, but they attack if they are scared and can bite a boat in two with their **powerful jaws** and **enormous teeth**.

An **electric eel** can zap a 500-volt electric shock – enough to **kill** an adult human.

Snake bites kill over 100,000 people a year, and fewer than **5% of humans** live after they've been bitten by a **black mamba**.

About **600 people** every year are killed by **elephants**, crushed to death by their 16 tonne bulk.

. . . and **African lions** kill around 250 people every year.

Bye!